Love Song

A

collection

of

POEMS

BY

SOPHIA MICHAELS

EU Conformity Declaration

This product complies with the following safety regulations and standards to ensure consumer safety and product quality: Regulation (EU) 2023/988 of the European Parliament and of the Council on General Product Safety (GPSR): The Consumer Product Safety Improvement Act (CPSIA), Section 101. The Californian Safe drinking water and toxic enforcement act. (Proposition 65) EN71-Part 1: Mechanical and Physical Properties EN71-Part 2: Flammability EN71-Part 3 Migration of certain elements.

Published and Manufactured by Softwood Books
EU Responsible person: Maddy Glenn
Office 2, Wharfside House, Prentice Road, Stowmarket, Suffolk, IP14 1RD
www.softwoodbooks.com
hello@softwoodbooks.com

EU Rep:
Authorised Rep Compliance Ltd., Ground Floor, 71 Lower Baggot Street, Dublin, D02 P593, Ireland
www.arccompliance.com
info@arccompliance.com

Paperback ISBN: 9781068669712

Grateful thanks
To the fantastic
Elizabeth Tilbrook
and Philippa Stroud
for
both being so fabulous,
beautiful
and
supportive.
Great ladies to work with.
I couldn't have fulfilled
my dreams without
you.

Love

Sophia Michaels

Quiet and good natured, Sophia Michaels' humble upbringing deep in the Suffolk countryside, shaped a steely determination to encourage others to make a difference. Many people are living in their self-made prisons and don't have to. Her goal is to change that, by word, song, and radio. Her poetry being the platform of thought, mind, and human sensitivities. Sensitivities, of which we all mostly dismiss or deny ourselves, preventing us from moving forward in life without the perception of the consequences of what we should have done.

The message.

Prepare yourself as best you can, show up, and do what you can. Plant the seeds and something good will eventually come out of your efforts so Sophia says, even if it's not quite the result you expected. As they say, God laughs at our plans, and usually has an even better one.

Like most of us, Sophia has faced many setbacks, but each time has picked herself up, brushed herself off, and persevered, something that shines through in her many 'gifts,' her singing, her art or radio presence, but most of all, her love of poetry.

Of course, don't take our word for it. Join Sophia at one of her one woman shows of storytelling, anecdotes and poetry coming soon at a venue near to you.

Titles

Complete Me

You come to complete me with your odd ways
I see your face
Revealed differently
I complete you
As you complete me
But do I give you what you really want?
Are you free to complete yourself?
Will you remember me when your wild heart strays?
You came to complete us
In the cold light of day
You can now never go away
Because you came to complete me
And this is where the completion stays.

Here I Present

Here I present to you
Our deep love
Awash
With raw emotion
Written within the water
It falls from mountain tops
Cascading as ever
Escaping to another level
Over the edge
Our love
Written
Deep down
Within the water
Knowing no bounds
Or constraints
Clearly
Written
Within the waters
Being seen
Touched
And felt
And drenched
And hot
And cold
And wild
And free
And calm
And like the Venus'
Ascent
From the waters below
Never in beauty denied
Nor her spirit contained
For our love

Is forever
Written deep down
Within the water
Every single drop
Of it
As it
Until
That is
It
Evaporates
Or freezes
Our deep love
Forever
Written
Within
The waters
She arises
Emerges
Flowing and falling
Still, and delirious!
And here she
Presents to you.

A Need to Know

I've a need to know
Of many things from you
And from you only
Why
You come to me
As you do
See me
Love me
Pull me in all manner of directions
Leave me
As you do
Put me into a box
On your way out the door
'Ciao Bella'
Do I not fit the bill
Am I the bitter sweet pill
Do I thrill
Only in the physical;
Between you and me
They'll never be any recompense
And no release
From this long sweet and bitter torture
Well
That's what it is like for me,
The honeyed persuasion
All the way to!

I've

I've got to write about
Beautiful September
In all her voluptuousness
Her fullness
Her deliverance
Her warmth of being
To me
Her abundance is
Her sex
Of nature
She is the orgasm
Of the year
Her ripening
And giving
And her season
And her reluctance
To give in to the next
As still she craves those heady days of Summer
She being the mother of all giving
Yet
Sexy September
Lays down the Winter's rules.

For she wears the coat of opposing colours
Showing off her fruit
Knowing that it will rot soon upon the stem
Her full body
Bursting
Giving her best
With nothing held back
She opens up her delight
Sweet sexy wild succulent serene September
Hot juicy running

Steamy
Pleasuring heightened senses
The jewel in the crown of the year
The miracle
Now that the Summer has gone
She has the chance to shine in her own right
Knowing that
She'll soon be wearing a different coat
But for now
She'll give abundantly.

Parallel

He loitered lazily
At the door as he watched her
With wistful look in his eyes
As she walked on by
In the dazzling sunshine
That even she outshone
Always.
Mmmmm...... he enunciated, quitely

He admired her countenance
Great poise and elegance
And the way her dress clung to her body
As the sun stole a moment through it
Giving rise to glimpses of her feminine form beneath
Revealing her gentle curves
Her well shaped legs and the place where they meet.
Mmmmm.....

He watched her strong stride
Walk purposefully confidently
Yet serenely along the sunny street
Everything about her all calm and neat
At that moment he basked in her proud beauty
Her easy demeanour displayed from top to toe
Now complete her stylish way undeniable.
Mmmmm.....

As she turned the corner he observed her
Flinging back her luscious shiny hair
Throwing a familiar spirited look in his direction
As she looked for her lover
Now out of sight.
He began to weep

Inwardly.
Mmmmm......

As he could never let their secret escape
Into the world
Beneath her
For she
Venus
Had crossed the universe
From constellation to nebula
Without prompt or interaction
Without union.

Or implication
Without recognition
Without indication
As
Both planets passed
In parallel emotion.
Mmmmm......
He enunciated,
Oh, shit!!

Pixel

For now
You will remain in pixel
And off somewhere in cyberspace
On my mobile phone
PC
Samsung
And that's where you will live
And reside
In perfect picture resolution
With flat dimension
In the darkness
Until I choose to press the button
To let light onto your face
Your words will live in folders
With no voice
Yet displaying their true meaning.

I could upload you to any network I please
Send you down another wire
Optic cable
Cell net
I could enable any programme I desire
Open up another file
Convert to voicemail
Configure
Then delete, but
Until I choose to press the button
This is where you will live
With messages incomplete
What network did you say you were on?
I would like to download your details
Now!
Into a virtual reality.

Sing You to Me

I sing you to me
My song
If only you would hear my voice
You are my choice
You are my song
You are the stave
Upon which the notes live
The key of e
The f sharp
A minor in the major
A fortissimo
Adagio
Moderato
Tempo
I've lived and waited far too long
For you to come to me
Put your words into my song
So instead
I'll have to put my words into your song
And sing you to me.

The Muddied Waters

The muddied waters will come and go
All the rest of the days of your life
I'll have you know
They'll come as the tides ebb and flow
All the moments of your bitter sweet life
I'll have you know.

Each day these troubled waters bring strife
Taking darkness into the light
And testing times
And times that test
You to the limit
Beyond your depths will ensue.

Blocking out the once crystal vision
Clearness of thought
Your life's mission
Just when you thought
It could not get any murkier
That you would never escape the mire.

Never again to be inspired;
On the horizon appears a glimmer of light
A striking of the fire
A spark of hope
All your trusted dreams take flight
The waters clear.

All the rest of the days of your life
I'll have you know
The tides will ebb and flow
They will come and go
High or low
Into the depth and shallowness
Limitlessly.

Perplexities

I watched you stride away
Purposefully
Quite in a hurry were you
Totally different from the person you were moments
before
What you had been in those moments
Just spent briefly snatched together again
I noticed you were slightly agitated as you strode hurriedly
away
From my concerned gaze
I wondered then about your perplexities
As the complexities of the days' events
Threw their worry across your eyes
And your brow
Showing on your face
Now transfixed on some business problem
I wanted to get inside your head then
To see what was really going on in your mind
But
As usual
The timing was all wrong
As there again
Were already so many perplexities.

If Only

If only the sun could burn the clouds away
Then what really lives beneath
Would be revealed
You being the complex clouds
In their many forms
Never the twain meeting
You being the clouds
She being the sun
And
Had you not been there
You would still be the clouds
And her
Always being the sun.

Corner of Your Eye

I see you
I see that smile
You have for me
Only for me
From the corner of your mouth
As it turns up slightly to one side
One small smile playing about your lips
On seeing me
I love that
Because I know it's just for me
Knowing then that you are watching me surreptitiously
Out of the corner of your eye
With that sometimes sideways glance.

I see you adjusting yourself
Across a crowded space
The cluttered room
Out of the corner of my eye
When you think that I am not looking!
In fact there is nothing. I do not miss about you
Out of the corner of
My eye
It touches me amuses me deeply
That I have this effect on you
As we apart and together we
Study one another out on the
Periphery.

She Loved

He touched the beauty of her body
And she loved it
He touched the firmness of her
She loved it
He caressed the heavenliness of her being
And she loved it
He held her strongly in the moonlight
She loved it
And smelt the scent of him
She loved it
As the scent of him lingered on her
She loved it
She loved it
Because it reminded her of him in all his gloriousness
She loved it
Because those memories of him
Will never fade
And she loved the, lingering!

My Love

My love will always be the same for you
I will always feel the same way about you
My body will always ache for you
My feelings will always want you
My spirit will always be enjoyed by you
My skin will always seek that special touch from you
My beauty will always radiate for you
My love will never change for you
And the perfection of our union
Will always be the decision of you.

Dangerously Beautiful Colours

The dangerously beautiful colours
Are all lies to our eyes
The deceptive creations entice
Fanciful hindering involvement
That's yours alone not mine.

Flippancy flourishes in you
But seriousness is what I need of you
You float upon your iced blue sea
I lie upon the intense red
And hell you still enter my head.

I see fire and what do you do
With your iced blue
You dampen my intense red
Until I am practically dead then you grip my arm
Enticing me to those heavenly white clouds.

Blissful intense red is what I now see for me
But for you it's still the iced blue
Now it's my turn
To turn grey
Because you say I must stay away.

I rise the lightning strikes
Thunder bolts through my heart
It crackles
An electric blue now enters your head
Surely you must want me anything but dead?

Your sentiments are strong indeed
Resolute you now must be
You shall see
I will redeem all
You have taken from me.

But now you are dead
So too is my intense red
And I shall never forever let
Dangerously beautiful colours again
Enter my head.

A Balance

When first
The falls of love
Caressed my youthfulness
Laughed I
Full of anticipation
And expectation
The softness
The grace
Mixed me up with smiles
And radiance which was
Not seen amongst the most
Who live not in the May
I sought and seeking
Got what I wanted
And needed
A feeling pimpled my skin
Emotion piercing the heart within
And love
Leaving its thoughtfulness
Forever in my passion
Struck down not
What thought I
You taught me that love could be a fall
A dull word upon a page
An eclipse in the middle of the day
A sparkle the coal could take away.
And the years passed in and out
The dark and light
The day and night
Need not send away the music
Of the feelings of love
Sexing me up
Catching me upon the unguarded moment

Sweat run dripping
My love ripping
And I was satiated.
In an unsatisfying balance.

The Garden

Do you like my garden darling
Is it not the most beautiful creation you have ever seen
Exquisite
A place to be in
A pretty scene
A perfect space
All serene
And what about the scent of it
As it fills the early evening's warm air
Filling your mind
As it lingers all about your senses
In unforgettable perfusion
My fertile hot sunny secretive spot
It's the only place to be in!
Do you like my garden, darling!

And How

He touched the beauty of my body
And how could I not have loved that
He touched the firmness of me
And how could I not have loved that
He caressed the heavenliness of my being
And how could I not have loved that
He held me strongly in the moonlight
And how could I not have loved that
I smelt the scent of him
And how could I not have loved that
The scent of him lingered on me
And I loved it
And I loved it
Because it reminded me of him in all his gloriousness
And how could I have not have loved that!
Because those memories of him
Will never fade
And how could I not love that.

Steel and Velvet

He is the concrete
And the cotton-wool
The feather
And the brick.

The cool glass
The searing heat
The moon
And the sun.

The wet
And the dry
The jagged edge of the precipice
The rolling hills.

The desert
The soft green grass
The roughness
The smooth silk.

He is the Angel
The Dark Knight
The fantastic heavenly light
The abyss in the ocean.

He is the foundation on the rock
The fall and rise of my breath
My strength
My weakness.

My ruby wine
The cheap lemonade
The calm
And the chaos.

My loss
And my gain
My fullness
My spirit drained.

He is everything that is not
He is not everything
The difference
And the same.

He is the harsh voice
The sweet song
He is my right
And my wrong.

My short
My long
My in
My out.

My shout
And my silence
My tears of course
My laughter.

The shallowness
The depth welled
My diamond
A piece of coal.

He is the commencement
And my cessation
The nail hammer
And the paper.

My porcelain cup
The clay pot
The antique
And the new.

He is the meek
And the wild
The first
And the last.

He is my listening ear
My deafness
The clothed
And unclothed.

The melting
And my solidity
The wholeness of me
And the emptiness.

To me he is everything
Opposite and the same
My sparkle
And the dullness.

My misery
My pain
My bloody annoyance
The ultimate sweetness.

To me his is what he is meant to be
Like myself to him
He is the give
And the take.

My sleep
And my wake
The real
And fake.

The heaven
And the hell
The beauty
And the shame.

Who is he to me
Who am I to him
I am to him
What he is to me.

Could this be me
Could this be him
Could this be I
Could this be myself.

To me he is everything
And the same
He will never remain
Always.

He is the time on the clock
The moment standing still
The here
And the gone.

He is my life long
My afterlife
My soul
My searching.

The ring
The wound
My healing
And my bleeding.

This is my finish
He is my start
And if we continue
That will be that.

But could he be
To me
The steel
And the velvet?
Perhaps.

Cling

I cling to you
But know not why
I cling
Like the food clings to the plate
Like folds to silk
A picture to the wall
The cushion to the chair
A lover to the bed.

I cling as summer to a flower
A rain shower freshly clinging to the lawn
The sun clinging to the dawn
The stars clinging to their brightness
Resentment clinging to anger
I cling to you
Like I wish that I did not.

I can't say goodbye
I can't run away
To greet the light of another day
Somewhere off many miles away
I cling to the voice of you
The one within
And to promises said
But really all I want to do
Is cling to the idea and voices I have in my head
Like sparkles clinging to a diamond.

I cling as a multi facet
A wrinkle to the skin
A problem to a wall
Ink to the paper
I cling lovingly as coldness to a stone

A river to the bank
I cling like kisses to lips
A bullet that does not miss

I wish that I did not cling
Like time to a clock
A softness clinging to a feeling
A ghost clinging to the past
Like a bride clinging to perception and anticipation
A last breath clinging to life
A man clinging to a dying wife.

The dullness of you clings to me
Like a thick fog clinging to a cold grey mountain
A dark ocean clinging to a dark shore
In the blackness of night
The thoughts of you cling to the back of my eyelids murkily
Like old clung up wine on the sides of the empty glass.
At the end of another bleak day with you.

Knowing You

You don't know me
But I want you to know me
If you want to
And I do want you too

Wherever you go
In the throws of your day it's
Not my way
That's for sure.

I wanna hear you
Knocking at my door
Demanding my presence
And company.

I don't want you to be living your life
Away from me any more
Never seeing my real light shine
Whatever the time.

Knowing you is all I want
But you won't know me yet
As I know you
As I have done so for sometime now.

Elemental Fashion

I'll let you be the power of the breeze sweeping over me
And in a moment be the rain inflicting the beauty
and the pain
The sun illuminating my space
You are the power
And that's all you'll ever be to me
That will be everything
And that will be nothing
In an elemental fashion
The wild water
And the passion.

You'll be the ignition of the fire deep within the
Very being of me
The sea set free
Leaving its constraints
You are the power
And force unseen
The elemental embrace
And that's all you will ever be to me
Nothing more
Not a thing less
Than the blue sky vast
The night sky's mystery
And the
Nights ripping by
Turning
In elemental fashion.

Time

Time takes us away
From
At this moment in time
And when that time returns
Time will take us away
To that place
And at that moment
All that we thought lost
Time takes us away
To our own space and time.

Time Slot

I'll be your lover
She said
And I'll do anything you want me to
Just as long as it fits in with your time slots
Diary
And schedule
Your day time rounds
And breaks in your day
All manner of events
That must coincide.

I came along
Just at the right time
During a transition in your life
She said
I'll be your lover for all time
Tonight
Today
Next year
And all the rest of the days of your life
She said.

But right now
She asks
Do you
Have a moment or two for me
Just now
Do you have a minute to spare
Could you possibly
Fit me into a time slot
She requested
Today?

Her Ways

I always knew there was more to her
Than met the eye
My eye
Way more
Than she let on
It was in the way her head swung round.

As she flung a glance in my direction
The way she set her eyes upon me
Holding steadfast my gaze
Smiling their uniqueness into me
Without word or say
Her look then told me all.

Well so I thought
In her fascination
Her ways
Reaching into me
Enigmatically
Her secrets.

And that very completeness
She displayed
She conveyed
She noticed the way
You looked upon her skin
Admired her subtle grace.

And the intensity of your observation
As you watched her mouth move
As she lured you in
With her charm
Appeal
And dreams.

Enticing you to her ways
She
On the other hand
Always knowing that
There was more to herself than met your eye
As this was always her way
And these ways will forever be her ways.

The She Wind

Your love of her
Brushes
As if wind against the grass
The wheat and barley move briskly
As the wind dances past
The rustle of the wind on a leaf
Is felt but never grasped
Unseen touching you
Everything around from above to the ground
Leaving everywhere devastated.

You'll never forget the wild wind being there
Its movement upon your skin
Its interrogation through your hair whilst
Shaking your hand on its way along the path
And when it has gone
And all is hushed and still
You'll sit there in your silence
Wondering where it all went
Why it is suddenly
So calm.

All quiet
Beautifully
Gently serene
And then it will come rushing back to you
In a storm
Blazing a hurricane through your thoughts
Tearing at each and every root of your hair
Ripping the soul out of the very air
Flinging wide your emotions
Never for one moment letting you forget.

Her
Power
And presence
Her rawness
Her soul
Her roaring tornado
The
Disturbia
Of
The she wind
Of it all.
'

And when it's all quiet again
All too calm
All too serene
Not one whisper heard
Everything unruffled
Peaceful and placid
Tranquil and soundless
Uninteresting
You'll wish
She
The she wind was there.

You'll shout,
Agonisingly
With your head clutched in your hands
I wish
I wish
She
Her
The total woman I love
The beautiful one
Was here with me.

And now
As in your daily life
You move from place to place
Hour by hour
You'll remember her
As the twisting wind dances past
You'll miss her heart beat
You now without her
Will be incomplete
And you will never again
Hold her
The she wind
For you allowed her only a fleeting memory
In your, short life
As the she wind danced past.

As Before

I can now never sleep as before
Without knowing your face
My hand tracing the lines upon it
Without the beautiful love you emanate
When I am with you
Your ways kiss me awake
My soul
Taking me to that perfect place.

I can now never sleep as before
Without your touch understanding my body
And its ways
Away from the light
Your ways
Feeling me
With your embrace
That envelops me.

I can now never love as before
You took me to the more
From the less
To a different shore
Out to realms new to me
Different spheres
Elevations
And inclinations.

I can now never cry as before
You seduced me with your charm
Your smooth operation
Your purposeful persuasion
Alluring talk
Seemingly
In your fascination toward me
In the very scheme of things that came.

I can now never look at you as before
You made the sadness in my life
My everyday embrace
The clothes I now wear
The style I exude
Charmingly
The many fashions living upon my face
My bohemian encase.

Are you that different
Darling
From what you were before?
Well
This is where I want all things us left
In this moment
Now
I can never be as before.

Soul Self

You are my soul self
My twin soul
My very self
A mirror
A flash
A glimmer
And hope
I win with you
Then lose my inspiration
The battle never ends
Between me and you.

You are my face
And surface
My longing
And certainly the indifference
To you I wear a shield
Then an openness
Not revealed
A lock down of my safe
Harbour in the turbulence.

You are my soul self
The person never been
Or gleaned I'd hope I'd become
The niceness never done
The calm and iciness
And the mix and match
The hotness and light
The confusion in the setting night injects
An apprehension into my insight.

A Smile

The scent of him
Danced about my moistened lips
Glistening in the softly lit memories
Misted in my mazy mind
That
Brought a smile to my mouth
As I remembered
Him.

Have You Ever Been There

There

Have you ever been, there
There
There
There
There
No stopping
There
Stay
There
Like this
Forever
Have you ever been there
In that place
That secret place
A clandestine space
Gentle
Hushed
Silenced
Quietly intense
In that moment there.

Don't tell anyone
But I hope you've been there
Like me
Greeted that moment there
Head on
Collision
Realising, at last that there's nowhere else to go
And that there's nowhere else you want to go or be
No other moment in this life for you to be in
Only in this moment do we live
I can't tell you what it's really like for you
That place

There
For you will know when you have been there.

It's the storm in the sunshine
A move upon my skin
A rich voice escaping
A depth of pleasure within
The vibration
A beauty beyond words and measure
It's a place like no other upon this earth
It's fireworks
Exploding in my brain
A diamond in creation
A touch like no other.

I never wanna leave this place so deeply felt
For it is never to be forgotten
Its memory leaving a lasting impression
A mark
Upon my whole inner being
In every vein
In my head
In every drop of sweat dripping from my body
And as you leave me
I want you to take me back
There
I'll whisper
Have you ever been there?

Linger

Let me gaze upon your face
A few seconds longer
That I may remember it a moment longer
Let me remember your touch
Even though at times it was all too much
Though in reality it was never enough
Let me stand before yourself a second longer
That I may smell the scent of you
So that its power and presence will linger
Forever
In myself.

Crowded Space

I've been across a road
A street
A crowded room
And seen your face
And your body
The face of the body
I've never had
The face of the body I always wanted
But as yet I've never had
But I will
But for now
My wonderings are still.

I'll know the moment your eyes strike mine
The moment their mirror reflects mine
The moment that smile plays about them
Then
Their innermost thoughts will be revealed to me
I've seen your body and your face
Across a road
A street
And the pleasure that passed came and ended all too soon
For I could not get across that crowded space
I could not get a moment
To caress and glide my fingers across your face.

A Letter As Promised

Every time I leave you
I want you more
Every time I want you more
I wish that I did not
Every time I ask and want you
To want me more
I wish that I had never asked
Or made the mere suggestion
Because every time I want you more
It appears to me that you do not want me more
Then every time you reject me
Then I am
Sorely hurt
To the bottom of my feelings that live within my body
Crying out for you to love me more
But I wish that I did not.

I love you more than the sun that loves my skin
But wish that I did not
I love you more than the flowers need the rain
But wish that I did not
I love you more than the snow blanketing the mountain
top
But wish that I did not
I love you more than a caressing wind on my face
But wish that I did not
I love you more than more than love itself
But most of all
I hoped and wished that I did not
But I will love you always
For as long as the picture of your face lives in my head
But
Most of all I wish that I did not

Believe
I went to the supermarket
With no particular thought in my head
And what do you think
I bumped into an old acquaintance
Whom I had no particular thoughts about either way
But
I could not believe the words he spoke to me
The words that tumbled out of his mouth
Falling surprisingly onto my eardrums
I was taken aback
I was shocked
But flattered all the same
I could not believe the way he looked at me
Standing so close to me
Smiling so handsomely at me
Why had he not told me this before
He said he could not believe
How well I looked
How good I looked
And what a lovely mouth I have
He could not believe my age
I could not believe my reaction
The words that spilled out of my thoughts
Escaping my lips
Landing upon his eardrums
Rioting through his veins
He was taken aback
But flattered all the same
He said
Why did you not tell me these things before?
Well
I replied
I just needed to believe.

The Voice

He was the voice I chased
The love I laced
The words I embraced
When I was entranced by his love
The difficulties displaced.
His voice was the one I heard in my head
As I lay in my bed
Wishing that sleep would come to me
Beneath the sheets
To rest the living wild thoughts I had running in my mind
He was the voice I chased
The love I laced
The truth of it I faced
Before love's voice shook me around!

Clouded Sunglasses

To me
You come like a cloud in the afternoon
Like rain
Like hail in torrents
You come like a cloud before the storm
The horizontal rain
And then with lightning and thunder
Blackening the day
You come to pull me up
Then under your spell deep dark and low
Loving me with your atmospheric moods
Inclement
Enigmatic ways
Your drive
And force
In all manner of conditions.

And then
After all this the
Clouds clear
Bringing the heat and light
Barometric pressure rising
I see the sun and sky and beyond
Revealing at last the stratosphere
The bright stars beyond
The birds soaring
Love exploring
A completed cycle
In a complex depression
Of crazed patterns
My clouded sunglasses suddenly clear
To bring about a more favourable forecast
At last.

Love

If a minute was an hour
And an hour a day
A day a week
A week a year
A year a century
A century a thousand years
A thousand years a millennia
My love would for you would last forever
In amougst the stars
In some far off sparkling constellation.

Ironic

It's ironic is it not
That you should laugh
And I should not
Through the pain and the hate
Through the love and the grace
It's ironic is it not
That you should laugh
And I should not.

Where I Go

Will you ever go where I go
Visit the places the same
Will you ever be where I've been
See the things that I've seen
Dream the same dream?

Will you ever go where I go
Feel the heat of the sun on your skin
On the very same day as me
Will you ever go where I go
Laugh the same laugh?

Will you ever go where I go
Dance on the same floor
Walk through the same door
To the cinema to escape
Cry at the same movie?

Will you ever go where I go
The restaurant
Leave a space at the table next to you for me
Drink from the very same cup
Ache for me the same?

Will you ever go where I go
The place where I don't go
The place where we could both go
To meet by chance and embrace for show
Know the meaning of the secrets on our faces.

Will you ever go where I go
To greet the love that sparks across a room
In a crowd of many
In leaping expectation
Steal the moment?

Will you ever go where I go
At the fall and rise of the sun
The pretence of the moon
Be there in the dark night for me
Catch a glimpse of the stars in agony.

Will you ever go where I go
And wonder how I in my exasperation
Greet the light of another day
Without you
Coming my way.

I hope
I cry
I feel
That you will
Go where I go.

After Love

After love
All quiet
And still
After love
Soft lines
And silk voices
After love ambience changed
From what it was moments before
After love
After our love
Hushed
And misted realities fade
Momently
As silence
Fills the day's chaotic spaces
Shifts our thoughts to different places
For some while
A moment or two
Loves wings takes us off to various realms
Graces never entered rooms
Not before entered or explored
These beautiful magical minutes preciously adored.

After love
Our love
After all our love
Now satiated
Hush
I love
The silence
You give to me
The gentleness
And peace

Quiescent
Serenity
Contentedness
Mocking all my moments
The deep beauty from within
For the harmony
And tranquillity
Is about to disappear
Again
As without hesitation
You walk calmly out the door
After love.

Tuscany

The scenery
Stunning.

The night sky
Extraordinary.

The storms
Spectacular.

The sun
Gloriously hot.

The surroundings
Dramatic.

The house
Another world.

Tuscany
A place to die for.

The roads
An experience.

I'll come here again
And again and again.

The fireflies
Enchanting.

The solitude
Reflective.

A Venus
In isolation.

A goddess
In contemplation.

The Day That We Are

The day that we are
Dust
And sand
And ash
And stone
You.

We will at last
Be the same
As each other
Together
Fused
Not different.

You'll move around our lovely planet
Over grass
Across seas
Transverse rivers
Canopy the trees
Live in the clouds above me.

You'll move around the earth
On the wind
On the air
You'll live in each storm and painful rain fall
And snow fall
Wherever you go.

I shall go
And wherever I go
You shall go
And then
You'll be the same as me
And you'll be ever the same.

As me
And this will be my comfort
For at last you are
Where you are meant to be
The day that we are melded
Per sempre.

Ethereal Dream

To her you are the water running warm
Along every strand and length of her soft hair
Which you always loved to comment upon
Your hand being the rise of the hot sun on her
The feeling of your hands caressing her as
Softly as honey running along her body
You are the press of the wind along her brow
The berry kisses on her sweet sensuous mouth
And the appreciation of her silkiness
Upon which you breathe your melting words.

You are her ethereal dream
The pristine
Love
Untainted untamed and for now
Unseen
She is the scattered oceans of the earth
Upon which the storms will come and ride
Landing on the shore
At your feet
She is the heat in the freezing snow.

She'll be there when there is nowhere else to go
When there is nowhere else for you to go.
She is the meandering in your veins
The river flowing per sempre
To her you are the tick tock chiming away the never
ending minutes
On the clock
Never ending minutes away from you
Those never ending minutes away from her
The next minutes on the day
The minutes gone and past.

There passing here only for a second or two
Momently for that matter
Before moving off to the future
In whichever direction
Minutes that will never come back this way
More minutes in her life stolen away
From her
By beautiful you
Her ethereal dream
Have you ever looked upon her
Seeing the real
And immaculate ethereal dream?

Dark Diamond

You shine
Sparkle
But I can't see the sunlight through you
Your multi facets always hidden
I cannot see your prismatic view
Your multi colours are like coal
Yet, your fire burns within me
Still you ignite me
You are the seat of the flame
My constant ire.
You don't speak to me as a sparkling gift clearly
For that's not what you want
It's not in you to do that
And you'll never understand what you are
You
The dark diamond
Shining like the midnight sky
To me you are nothing else
You are not the shine or
Scintillation
Or there to be my dream
My wish
My precious gem
To me
You are
Just
A
Dark diamond.

A Special Gift

To me you are a special gift
To be unwrapped
Slowly
Layer by layer by layer
And
Lovingly
To be savoured
Admired
And
Adored
Trouble is
I can only have a very small piece
To love
And appreciate
To whisper upon
Ti amo
At a time
Then
All too quickly
I must
Return the gift
To the now very crumpled
Wrapper.

Since You

Since you enveloped me
My winters have never been the same
I do not feel the coldness
The snowflakes bitter beauty
Their feathery touches as they fall upon my skin
I've not since you wanted to see much else
To feel or touch the ugly things
Like normality
In life
I've seen only
Lovely things
Since you.

The Flames

My love for you dances
As the flames in the hearth
Warm me;
With their clinging heat
And colour
Some blue
Some red hot
And sun rise orange
Differing one moment to the next
They flicker;
Changing shape
One second to the next;
Blush contours I cannot grasp
Nor am I quick enough to catch
Their individual image
In my eye
I just know that the beauty is there
As glimpses tantalisingly shift form
Without stop or start.

Passing Through

You're just passing through my life
Right now
In my life to take notice
Right now
And for the moment
You'll be there
In my hair
On my skin
And across my vexed brow
Being in the questions that live in my eyes
Your movements dancing about me
Teasing me
Right now.

Playing with me
To what was is
And could
Become
Right now
As you pass through my life
Right now
For the time being
And then the next out of it
You could be gone in a flash
As quick as a dash
As quickly as turning off the light switch
Leaving me to where I was at before
You
Right now.

The Glass

I pressed my lips to the rim of the glass
You had just drank from
I caught the faint scent of you on it
Sending my thoughts back
To the moments before.

You drank the sweet liquid
Enjoying every sip
You took
Down to the very last drop
From the glass.

I could see the joy
Crazed across your handsome face
As you run your fingers over the smoothness of it
And the coolness of its shape
As it intoxicated you.

Mmmm, I heard fall from your mouth
As you eyed me from your seated space
Come darling lets fill the glass again
Go back to that magical place
Back to the orgiastic heaven.

Me

I passed by the place
Where once you stood
Looking at me
Laughing with me.

I felt that I was the only person in the room
I was the only object to look upon
Your desire
Back then.

I felt as though
I was the only thing you ever wanted
To see
The voice you wanted to hear.

And the delightfulness you sought
I was everything in that moment
And many things in your life
And then you took yourself away from me.

You were then out of sight
Mind
And touch
With no connection being made.

No communication
No conversation
No room for confrontation
And no mediation.

That room now being void of you
And all the presence you ever had
Now lives in another place
And new space.

Away from me
Without me and not in my space
Every look you ever flung toward me
Your obvious longing vanished!

The way you reached for me
Articulated lavish words
On me
Now faded to the past.

But now you are gone from me
And the space where once you stood
Exists as if you had never ever been there
In the first place.

I was everything you wanted
Everything you ever dreamed of
In your life at that moment
Then when that moment in your life

Came and ended and had gone by
It was time for you to say
Goodbye.
To me.

Deliver

The stars shoot by
When you deliver
Out of your normality
When you have left the minds of your day
The other stuff that clouds and gets in the way
And stacks up in your head.

And when the stars have shot by
Your minutes before are forgotten
You take us right out of the sky to the unusual
Right away from a familiarity
To another place.

I lay waiting
For those minutes to return
When you shoot by
In the hope
That I will
Deliver
With you
Once more.

Toy

You toy with me mea cara
And my ideas
As you do
You hurt me
Causing me pain
And yet more angst.

The way the days pass by
With you
Are a whirl
And a fantasy
But still you toy with me my dear
Mea cara.

The games you play
Are all but ways to score points
Marks upon a board
A strike recorded on a card
The final match
You toy with me mea cara.

You leave me waiting
To play the next match
The next game, and
Waiting for me to play ball
As you enter the arena
In the hope that you'll win
Mea cara.

Having the advantage
This time.
Mea cara.

Stand

I'll stand with you
Alongside you
As long as you want me to
In my understated way.

I'll hold into and onto your hand
I'll uphold your ideas
Give to them thought and light
I'll be your sanctuary.

I'll be before you
I'll be what you thought I was
I'll always be that way, for you
And you'll always be to me exactly what I thought
you would be to me.

Linger No longer

I'll let you stand before myself
As you set your eyes upon my face, and
I'll show you all the beauty you want, and the grace
I'll let you linger there for a few seconds longer
As I flick my hair by your presence
With the swift action of my hand
That you may catch the scent of me
As I linger tantalisingly
In that secret inner space
That lives
Between me and you
And then I'll let you gaze upon my face
A few seconds longer
Before I escape
To linger no longer.

Linger II

Let me hold on to your hand
A few seconds longer
That I may feel the strength of you
As you take me through to you.

Let me look at you more than a moment longer
A few seconds longer
That I may caress your beauty and depths
With my eyes.

Let me love you again, observe
Your look toward me
Taste your life
Breathe my words of love into you.

Let me be the song within you
The cry you hear in the night
The constriction in your throat
These being the reminder of who I am to you.

As our days pass by
Look at me a few seconds longer
That you may remember
My countenance and charm
And, my lingering look.

With You

Walk beside me
All the rest of the days of your life
Mea cara
Be my guiding light
The love upon which
I will rest my soul.

With you there is no ugliness
No horrors
You take it all away
You make me whole
You make my life
Molto amore.

Be the wind pushing through my hair
My sweetly scented hair
I want you there
Where it all really matters
Where really you should be
Per sempre

Be the dress I wear upon the summers evening
My dress clinging to my moistened skin
As the dusk creeps across the horizon
Linger over me
With me
Bellisima.

Hold my hand
Stand by me
Run with me
Win the race
Reach into me
With me.
Ciao.

The New Level

Take me to loveliness
Down into its softness
Make me whole
Make me complete
In that warmth
That energetic heat.

I wanna be everything to you
The sun
The rain
The soft grass beneath your feet
The dewy morning greeting you
And I'll be your pain.

If you'll let me
I'll be everything to you
Add to your life a new jewel
For you to appreciate
And accept
For I will be to you
A, new level.

Am I

Am I your greatest love
And yours

Am I your lilly Langtry
And you my Edward

Am I the great light
And you my sun

Am I the stars
And you the night

Am I the pen
And you the paper

Am I the touch
And you the feel

Am I the melody
And you the lyric

Am I your Cloepatra
And you my Anthony

Am I the share in your life
Am I the will I be the ever

Am I the very intimate
You want to be

One question
Am I?

A Facet

I discussed with you
A facet
Or two
About things between me and you.

The missing things that were never there
Your feelings never quite true
As I imagined
Between me and you.

At the same time
Pieces here and there
All these things that keep me wishing
That there was always just one other part to add.

Another component
And at least one more facet to cut
And aspect
Another piece that might draw it all together.

The things
Between me and you.
I thought I was your dream come true
As discussed with you on an occasion or two

Your completion
Well that's what I saw was in my mind's eye.
But alas not.
I was just another point.

In your life
Without
Conclusion
A strand twisted.

Not entwined
Or anchored
Or attached and
Never intertwined
Or secured were these things between me and you
should have been.
I was just the thing between me and you.

Cup Cake

I must be after a fashion
A cup cake
All sweet and runny
Fragrant
Multi fruited
Colourful
And tasty
Lucky you!

A dreamy mixture
Of icing sugar
A sultana
Here and there
A fancy
A French one at that
Smelling sweetly nice
And delectable.

I could be chocolate dark
And light
Smooth hot
Bubbly
Stirred up to max
Frothy and
Cloying
With a taste never forgotten.

Lucky you
For finding me
A delicate interruption
To your day
An excitement
A syrupy introduction

A cherry laced interaction
A creamy liquidity.
Never found in any bakers shop
Ha, ah ha ah ah
Who loved the sweet taste
Ha, ah ah ah ah
Did you
Enjoy
Your
Cup cake
Darling?

Ah ah ah ah!

How Come

You come by
But never say good night
But you can say good bye
How come it's all so easy for you
With your charms
And good looks
Saying anything that you might think
I wanna hear
That will keep me at your knees
Keeping me where you please
And with what pleases you
The curl of your hair
And smile on your lips
Play on the slant
How come
And why
Do you
You come by?

Vanilla Spice

When
You want spice
You'll, come to me
I am wild
Baby
Free
I'll rock you
Around my bed
Put you into orbit
Shoot you right
Out to the stratosphere
Burst new stars into your head
I'll be the heaven in your love bed
And you'll love it
I'll be your vanilla spice
Sweetly aromatic
Unforgettable
Forever
Baby!!

Linger lll

I linger with you
Because I have to I linger
Because I want to I linger
Because I need to I linger
As sure as the snow
I'll never let go or
Give you wings
So you can take flight
From me
I'll make sure
You'll linger.

For the rest of your life
You will linger within me
You will never leave me and
In your mind
I will linger
Forever
In you
As you in me.
Where neither one of us can
Linger
One without
The other.

My Space

You're in my space
My face
You're in my blog
You're my twitter
Every time I press the button
You just pop right up as you do!
Onto my screen
From cyberspace.

You think you have the right
To invade my apps
My memory banks search engine
Interface
All you do is punch in a name
And up you pop Baby, and
Along with a thousand others
Just like you
Looking for the same things as you.

I could save you in my folders
Into draft form
Save you for another day
Download you
Open you up
As and when it pleases
At my leisure
When I have the pleasure time.

Put you into cloud
Facebook and
Last minute dot com
Trouble is
I've virtually no time

Of late with you
For you
So I'll just have to say
Goodbye
Then press
Control
Alt
Delete.

Black Butterfly

He watched her flutter by
The beautiful
Black Butterfly
Flit by.

In her shimmering dress
With her spellbinding ways
Her enigmatic illusiveness
Unparalleled.

He had never seen such loveliness
In all his life
Her enchanting ways
Encapsulated his heart.

Her light touches
Felt like whispers upon his skin
The dark wings
Glistering in the hot summer sunshine.

Her light touch leaving him
Breathless
Unable to utter one single word
She was all he had ever wished for.

All the days of his life
His dark life
As dark as her beautiful wings
Now taking flight.

As she fluttered by
He wanted to ensnare her
Catch her
Net her
And keep her

But he
Dared not.
She would then be
Beautifully
Lost.

Loves Ghost

I saw you standing
Staring at me
From the bar as I walked in
You beckoned me with a hand gesture
A smile
And the promise.

And I, like the fool that I am
Walked toward you enjoying the look of you
Drinking you up
The physical presence of you
As you appeared to me
That is;

Appealing to me
As well as
The strength of your aura
Magnetically drawing me in
To your inner sanctum.
Trouble is as soon as I, touched, you,
You disappeared like
Loves' ghost.

As Before

I can now never sleep as before
Without knowing her face
Feeling her breath upon me
Without the beautiful love she emanates
When I am with you
Her ways kiss me awake
Taking me to that perfect place.

I can now never sleep as before
Without her touch understanding my body
And its ways
Away from the light;
Her ways
Feeling me
With her embrace
That envelops me.

I can now never love as before
She took me to the more
From the less
To a different shore
Out to realms new to me
Different spheres
Elevations
And inclinations.

I can now never cry as before
She seduced me with her charm
Her smooth operation
Her purposeful persuasion
Alluring talk, all
Seemingly, in her fascination toward me
In the very scheme of things that came.

I can now never look at her as before
She made the sadness in my life
My everyday embrace
The clothes I now wear
The style I exude
The many fashions living upon my face
My bohemian encase.

Are you that different
Darling, she would say;
And this is where I want all things us left
In this moment
Now;
I can never be as before
You came to me.

At A Pace

You walked into the room with your usual pace
With consternation scribbled across your face
Like you had to win the race
Getting to that place.

You looked as though you were definitely on the case
And that was all you had to chase
And then you looked at me observing my poise and grace
As I sat so serenely in that space.

A smile softening across your face
Lowering your defence as you caught me tight in your embrace
Planting kisses upon my mouth and face
Our relationship as intricate and as delicate as lace.

Nothing about it easy to encase
Nothing about it easy to replace
Nowhere to put it in a permanent place
Not even in my space.

Out there in cyberspace
Where it might live in virtual space
Not easy to trace
No real way to deface.

What transpired between us at a pace
And now as I trace
The lines around your face
I realise with much disgrace

All I ever was to you
Will never live in real time and space

Detach with grace
Something that should never happened in the first place.

Along The Street

Along the street
She walks all neat
Head held high
Content by the blueness of the sky
As she walks on by your place
Hoping that you would set your eyes upon her face.

But as usual
You like nothing to confuse you
So you ignore her
But really you are looking at her surreptitiously
Out of the corner of your eye
Asking yourself why.

You let her go
In your angst and woe
You got what you wanted
You were besotted
And could never say no
To the beauty of her.

She now has left a scar
So big
It will never heal
Even if you were to come back to claim your prize
Thinking now that you can love her at every sunrise
She asked you to;

Watch her
As she walks on by
All neat
Along 'your' street.

Not In So Many Words

And now you have told her
That you'll never leave your life
That you will never come to her
You did not say these words directly
You did not say them out loud
You did not need to, she knew

For your actions spoke louder than your words
She heard what you were saying loud and clear
As you spoke them silently to her
As time went by
In your own connivance.

You only ever wanted to love her your way
She had no say
I have to say
In the very way
You wanted her to love you

And one day you will go from her
Away to your place
To look upon another face
Wishing it was hers
And that I was standing in that very space.

Well, darling
She is exactly
Where
You
Want her to be

Out of the way
Up the road

Along another street
Living her life
Without you
In her own way.
Ciao.

You

It's part of me
The way you live in me
It's where you are meant to be
You are the seed that lives in me
It always has.

It's the flowers bloomed
The night shone stars
A vein on the back of my hand
As the blood beats by.

You'll beat by
In your way
And pump up the volume
As high as it will go.

And as free as it will flow
Then you'll go
Back to your haunts
And listen to ya mates.

The Perfect Storm

Heaven was sent down to earth
When she came upon him!
She owned him the second her body hit the ground
Crash landed into his space. Boom

Her beautiful face
Her elegance
Eloquence
And style.

Her philosophy struck him
As she said
You know
We are only here once
So don't let me go

Because 100 years from now
We will all be dead
And who will give a fuck about what you and we did
Or said.

He had looked for her all his life
Her feel and touch
He had composed her nearness in his mind
Many, many a day

And for too many nights, many many days of his life
He had seen her in his minds eye
Wish she would fall out of the sky, Boom!
Well, what do you suppose, she did.

In all her ferocity and velocity

With warning signs being there sometime before
The seas had risen
Out of all recognition
The horizon had blackened

A hurricane had come
A tornado
Swept across the planet
All for the want of her.

She walked, across his life, Boom!
Exploded right in his face
Proud
Wild
Serene
Erotic
Difficult
Calm

Awesome
Graceful
Enigmatically
Alluringly
And tearful
Purposefully
Demanding his attention.

And always perpetually
Challenging;
The
Vortex in his head
With her as he always wished
The perfect storm had justly
Arrived

Well
Baby
You pays ya money
Baby
And
You takes ya chances.
Baby!
The beautiful tempest had come.
Boom!

But

They'll always be this, but
That hangs in the air
Between us
That hangs on every word
Every sentence I have ever written and said
Even though you may not hear it
It will be silently said
There'll always be this, but;

Behind every word I have ever spoken
Every action
And reaction
Between us
Behind every question
And statement ever mentioned
Rhetorically or otherwise
There will always be this but;

Between us
At every parting
And every meeting
Upon every greeting
And every fleeting disagreement
Composition, and
Decision.
They'll always be this big but;

But
Darling
Remember
One thing
But!!

Dissipate

You told me
That you went to bed
To
Perchance to dream of me
Dreams
Darling
What are these
I have far
Too many of them
So why not share a dream or two with me
Before they dissipate and
Lead
To nothing
But mist
And fog
Get the picture?
Clearly!

When I Love You

I can't wait for you to arrive
On my doorstep
The excitement
Almost bursts out of the door
And onto the street.

The anticipation of it all
Leaves me exuberant
Tingling
And ready
For you.

Then in you walk
You swagger in
Smiling
All lean
And eyeing me.

Then, when I love you
I'll lead you to this place
Belonging to no other
Out of reach to the outside world
A private special space.

There Is A Picture

I see you
But between us
There does not exist a picture
Nothing to look at
To appreciate
Not one piece of artwork.

Pointillism
Cubism
Or otherwise
The picture will only ever live within its own space
It will give out its own grace
Command.

Its own presence
In the room
It will say things about
Me
And
You.

How we were
And where we went
It will say
Give clues
About our lives
And where we lived.

The colour of our eyes
Skin tone
Laughter
Giggles and smiles
There were plenty of them

But now the time has come.

For you
To look at me
And to realise that I am the only one
And not just
Some one!
Out there.

This is how you make me feel
And see things
Darling
Mea cara
Molto amore
Per sempre.

Ciao.

Miniscule

I loved every minute part of you
With every miniscule part of me
With every slight movement
You ever displayed
Lives in the memory you helped to create
Nothing of it will ever be lost
Or will ever be able to escape
Not one speck
As I see now that our love
Was only ever
Atomic!

The Pea Jar

I kept it by the bed
The pea jar
And every time I made love to you
After you had left
I dropped a dried pea into it
And each time you came by to love me
I dropped another dried pea into it.

Wow, I thought at this rate
It would fill and empty the jar in no time
At all
Well that's what I thought and expected
As it filled up to the brim
Love after love
Your sex after my sex.

The jar lived on the bedside table
With me only to look at it
Realising the significance of it
The measure of the influence in my day
And the consequence of my night
It, the pea jar
Always being there in the morning.

Your position was not to be
In the midst of things to come
When the day was not quite done
And I was quite alone
In the scheme of the things to come
Trouble is they never lived
Together in
The pea jar and the emptiness.

Nipped in the Bud

Our love will never flourish under a tree
Bear flowers
Or ripened fruit
Perfume the air with sweetened scent
Impress with its beauty
And magnificence
And taste
It will only ever be but a bud
Wrapped in tight expectant constraints
And when the first frosts spreads its bitter coldness
Potentiality, will be nipped in the bud
And never having had the chance to unfurl
It
Will
Die.

When

When you go to your bed
Imagine her there
Her perfumed hair, draping
Silky skin, smooth
Soft murmurings' repeating
You all wrapped up in her

Her assailing scent
Her closeness
The mixing
And looks
Touches saying
Just one thing

Looks deep
And caresses on
Flushing glow
Tightness together
Compliant
Accepting.

Deep panting
From all below
Meeting at the surfaces
Beautiful moments
Hot and displaying
Vibration
All invigorating.

When you go to your bed
Imagine her
Glistening
And shimmering skin

As it sets on yours
Leaving a lasting impression
As you draw her deeply in
Breathing.

She asked
Give me one reason why
In your imagination
She is there
And you are not here
Only in your imagination
After all we seem to have shared
With beautiful one another.

The Sweetness Forever.

The impression I get
Alters from one second to the next
And I am vexed
As to why
I should question this again.

Your voice
Rich and mellow
With intent
Consumes me
Right down to my very sexual core.

Wow
It could not be the more
No less
How boldly exciting
I am sensual without shame.

I know you love this of me
The way I flex
My pliancy
My mind always
Defiant.

Though
After our meeting place
Has inspired
Ensued beyond our usual normality
And your frugality.

Harvests
The sweetness
A vibration here

One there
Presiding copiously in your memory.
Loveliness wasted going off
To some other lonely place
You leave me
Because you cannot convey yourself
Right permanently.

To live with my beautiful face forever
For I am outside your realm
And sphere.
I do not have the grace
To fill that ivy towered space.

In which you chose to reside
With your mind encased
Wishing you could command
My space
Set my pattern.
In duty
The same
My sweetness runs forever
Whether or not
I live within your constraints.

Get

Get your act together baby
It may be your last chance
Baby
For I'll soon be taking all it away
Taking me away
In my own way
Baby.

I'll tell you to be on your way, baby
Because all you want
Baby
Is your way
With me
Conveniently out of the way
Baby.

Up the road, baby
Not in your way
Baby
Not in your back yard
Being in your way
Spoiling your life's way
Marring your day baby.

I never thought baby
That you could be like you are
Baby
Selfish
Yet unassuming
To others all around
Baby.

Well I've got news for you baby

I spotted your game a mile off
Baby
Me being conveniently spaced away from you
Baby
I am no more prepared to be your
Baby.

Waiting
Baby
For you to cry wolf
And to get your act together
It is now my turn
Baby.

To turn the tables
Baby
And
To get my act together, baby
So from now on
Baby
You ain't no longer my baby.

The Picture

Today I am going to turn the page
To look at a different picture
As I am right fed up of looking at your picture
And what your picture says to me.

I've made up my mind at last that
I don't want to look at your picture any more
I
Need you to look at mine.

For once
For a change
And why should I look at your picture
When you can't be bothered to look at mine.

So from now on
When you ask me to look at your picture
To get a view of the bigger picture
I am going to say no.

Until you are prepared
To look at my bigger picture
And what it says to you.
Now do you get the picture?

Something for you to Remember.

When you love her
Remember
When you love her
Remember this
That she is not easy to forget
She never will be
But
Be warned
You
Might be easy to forget
Something for you to remember.
But,
She will not
Remember.

The Meeting Place

I cannot wait for you to meet me there
Once again
I remember the looks we share
Right well baby.

As there is never a may be
Between us then
I remember
In that room.

We often assume
The space
We call
Embrace.

We reach
Often
The smile
At our meeting place.

Intensifies
As the moments
Pass
Delightfully on.

Encased
Enveloped
Wrapped around each other
At
Our meeting place.

Showing Me Off

I can show myself off
Any time I like
Right!
But you can't me
Though you think you can
You cannot show me off at all
I don't need you to do that for me
And in any case
I am quite capable of doing it myself
I can show myself off any time I like
What about you baby!!!

Ya Mates

It's part of me
The way you live in me
It's where you are meant to be
For now;
You are the seed that lives in me
It always has
It's the flowers bloomed
The night shone stars
A vein on the back of my hand
As the blood beats by;
You'll beat by
In your way
Pump up the volume
As high as it a can go
As swollen as you like to take it
As free as it will flow
Then off you'll go
Back to your haunts
To listen to ya mates
Overflowing with ya smiles.

She Saw

She saw you
And she was wowed off her feet
All those years
Ago
She thought
Mmmm
And wondered where it would all go
If only he would look her way
And let go
Of the things familiar
Back then though
She did not realise
That often he would sideways glance at her
As she standing quite near to him in his personal space
But somehow she sensed he was looking intently at her
face
Studying her haughty countenance.
She knew he loved her unique look back then
So she was informed often, later
As he appreciated her more closely
No one else ever looked at her the way he did
As he so did, letting him into her personal inner space
Oh privileged one
She saw,
everything.
Then she had you wowed off her feet.

A Chance Meeting

A chance meeting all those years ago
When my life was full of woe
And yours to me seemed so perfect
With the angst in mine you failed to detect.

I looked up to your face
Observing your masculine grace
As you handed me the first look
That back then in disbelief I took.

I had walked right into your crowded space
It was then you had noticed my face
My haughtiness
My elegance and grace.

A darkness shadowed on my brow
As I realised wanted to deliver a kiss just then
Your intense gaze
Softened me right there and then.

Your attention to my detail
Enthralled my empty life
Your caress of words
Loved me back even then.

Before love dared enter our solar plexus
You entreated to me
That you wanted me
Without condition or encumbrance.

My beauty enlaced your mind
Encased your thoughts
Fingered your nerves
Got you thinking.

Did I back then wear the magnificence
In my dress
In the pace of my walk
And the quick turn of my talk.

You wanted me then
Your sweeping hand
Brushed every one aside
Except me.

For I had ignited life in you
A long unlit flame
A warmth
And a passion.

Your true love had just delivered
The love you had always wanted
But was always afraid to face
For I had now struck your inner peace.

And as now you reflect on me
As many a time in a secret place
With remorse shattered upon your face
You'll wonder and say to yourself.

I did nothing to deserve her
I could not keep her
She the Goddess
Empowered me.

At my peril
To face my demons
And to have courage
To live.

For her!!!
But now she is gone from me
I consume my days
In her total grace once given pleasure.

Her mannerisms
And vibrations
With regret
And emptiness, hollowness
A void is all that now fills her space.

The End
For
Now

Author's Note

My study is the voice of the life the joy and the pain of it, and its rawness. The observation and the questions of it, and that of which made me ask why we are here. To what point is the purpose of our being here in this existence, and frame. What guides us to where we go, and takes us away from what we love and know. What will we seek, and in it what will we find? How shall we deal with it, and the outcomes? Life is too short my beloveds.

This has been conveyed to me on the many occasions I happen to meet with friends for lunch. Where fantastic earthly conversations, in our very small way, took place on the grand scheme of things. To me, we are just bursts of dust on the breeze, streams of light from the sun, romantic ripples on the water, but written in the rain in the end, then blown away with the storm making our mark at land fall.

Life opens us up to the opportunities, possibilities and the fantastic things of yet to come. Yet, in the same breath these doors can slam shut in our faces, barring and locking us out, and from these experiences onward we will forever ask ourselves what happened.

And if I were to place a bet right now, I bet you would say to yourself:

I wanna live, and live I must now, before it's too late, and the gift of dreams are gone.

Now I Know the Place Where You Come From
Now

It is not me you come from
Now
Out of our love
Now
That is very strong
Now
I want you to know that
Now
And this
Now
It's the kiss you leave upon my lips
Now
The way you melt me
Now
With your own song
Now
And the way you sing it to me
Now
And the words written within the song
Now
The way I react to them
Now
The way they reach into me
Now
Then
Now
Tell me
Now,
How
I know the place where you come from
Now.

The End

The Second End

With A Few

Tweeks

Back Word.

My study is the voice of the life the joy and the pain of it, and its rawness. The observation and the questions of it, and that of which made me ask why we are here. To what point is the purpose of our being here in this existence, and frame. What guides us to where we go, and takes us away from what we know and love, and how we love. What will we seek, and in what we seek, and in it, what will we find. Will we find love? Whatever love is. Whatever is love? How shall we deal with it, and its outcomes. Life is short, and so can love be. This has been conveyed to me on every occasion I happen to meet with friends for lunch and fantastic earthly conversation, in the massive scheme of things, in our small way of things great. To me, we are but bursts of dust on the breeze, streams of light from the sun, romantic ripples on the water, but written in the rain in the end, then blown away with the storm making our mark at land fall. At Loves' fall!

Love, opens us up to the opportunities, possibilities and the fantastic things of yet to come. Yet, in the same breath these doors, can slam shut in our faces, barring and locking us out. From these experiences onward we will forever ask ourselves what happened.

And if I were to make a bet, I bet you would say to yourself.

I wanna live, I wanna love, and live I must now; before it's too late, and the gift of emotions are gone.

How many of us have said this ourselves?

Much Loveliness To You All
Always
Sophia Michaels

www.ingramcontent.com/pod-product-compliance
Lightning Source LLC
LaVergne TN
LVHW030636080426
835508LV00024B/3375